T0102150

little book of

PARiS
style

Aloïs Guinut is an author, personal stylist and image consultant. She is the author of *Dress Like a Parisian* and *Why French Women Wear Vintage*. She lives in Paris.

Published in 2022 by Welbeck
An imprint of Welbeck Non-Fiction Limited,
part of Welbeck Publishing Group.

Based in London and Sydney
www.welbeckpublishing.com

ISBN 978-1-80279-261-4

Printed in Dubai

10 9 8 7 6 5 4 3 2 1

ALOÏS GUINUT

little book of

PARiS
style

The Fashion Story of the Iconic City

WELBECK

CONTENTS

INTRODUCTION

Paris must be the only city whose female inhabitants are presented as singular rather than plural. "La Parisienne" – The Parisian – is the first image that springs to mind when talking about Paris style. An effortlessly stylish mythical being whose "just-got-out-of-bed" hair and jeans always look impossibly chic.

More than a female inhabitant of Paris, "La Parisienne" is an aesthetic. According to the writers of a recent bestseller, you can *Be Parisian Wherever You Are*. This approach applies both to a style and an attitude: possess a certain culture and wit, be (or at least *appear* to be) careless, wear the no-makeup look (but have perfectly pampered skin) and be stylish without being too loud – perfectly mainstream characteristics. Which excludes some actual Parisiennes being enthroned as "La Parisienne". Incidentally, Inès de la Fressange's book *La Parisienne* is a bestseller in Paris too, which says a lot, despite some Parisiennes simply not aspiring to this aesthetic.

The Parisienne style is praised for its restrained chic. Naturally cautious when it comes to new trends, Parisiennes tend to stick to what works best for them, although they will incorporate the shape, colour and print of the moment into their timeless outfits. It's a philosophy that makes them less prompt to buy the latest "hot" thing and in so doing, prevents the odd *faux pas*.

But a singular cannot encompass the globality of Parisiennes. Let's face it, most images we see in the media that claim

Introduction

Inès de la Fressange wears a leather jacket and red lipstick in Paris, c.1980.

to represent La Parisienne are of thin, bourgeois and white women. Indeed, I myself fit this description, as do the majority of those working behind the scenes in fashion and writing books about Parisian style, proving that there is an ongoing lack of opportunity in the fashion industry unless you fit this stereotype. However, since much-needed conversations on diversity have finally opened up, the sheer diversity of Parisian women is finally being platformed. On social media you can see a broad scope of women embodying Parisian style, such as influencers Fatou N'Diaye from Black Beauty Bag, plus-size model Clémentine Desseaux and YouTuber Léna Mahfouf, and, in the mainstream media, entrepreneur and TV host Hapsatou Sy. *Vogue France* has finally broadened the spectrum of girls introduced in the viral *"une fille, un style"* (a girl, a style) videos. Brands such as Sézane and Jacquemus include diverse models in their campaigns and shows, while designer Ester Manas has created an acclaimed size-inclusive brand.

So, does this "Parisian style", one described in countless books and articles, really exist, you might wonder. Well, some Parisiennes fit the aesthetic so perfectly, they are invited by leading magazines to share their "secrets". And it cannot be denied a style vibe still emanates from the city as a whole, despite fashion globalization. Indeed, Paris radiates effortless chic. By day or night, the crowd is quite dressy (you will see very little sporty attire), while never over the top (loud styles are not a common sight). Some clichés also prove to be true, as a quick glance at a bunch of Parisians dressed in subdued shades and regular encounters with stripes confirm. The aim of this book is to understand how this specific Parisian style was born and what it is now through the designers, fashion icons, mythical staples and all the small habits that forged it.

Eight models posing on the set of *Under the Paris Sky*, 1951.

Street style at Paris Fashion Week, October 2020.

Birth of La Parisienne

Paris and its surroundings have long been setting trends in France and the rest of Europe. In the 1600s, those closest to the King were setting the newest trends. In the next century, Marie Antoinette's rural style was followed by women eager to trade voluminous gowns for simpler models.

After the French Revolution, Versailles was no longer at the centre of it all. The Republic, the Restoration monarchy and then the Empire all settled in Paris. With the Industrial Revolution, the fashion economy was booming. With its rich history of manufacturing fabrics such as silk in Lyon and lace in the North, France was one step ahead. At that time, "Les Parisiennes", plural, referred to all women living in the city, whether of modest means or upper class, who shared a love of elegance and seduction. Meanwhile the designer Charles Frederick Worth transformed couture into an art. Established in Paris, the Englishman offered his wealthy clients designs they could customize, placing himself as the creator where previously tailors were mere executors of style.

The first iterations of "La Parisienne", singular, emerged in the mid-1800s. In 1841, the journalist Taxile Delord penned an article titled "*Physiologie de la Parisienne*" illustrated by a beautiful young woman surrounded by admirers. "The Parisienne is a myth," he wrote. This elegant and seductive *bourgeoise* also became the subject of paintings by Renoir and Manet. In 1900, an elegantly dressed giant statue of La Parisienne by Paul Moreau-Vauthier welcomed visitors to the Paris-based world fair, turning this French myth into a global one.

Introduction

Marie Antoinette in a Chemise Dress by Élisabeth Vigée Le Brun, c.1783.

English fashion designer Charles Worth (1825–1895) working at his salon in Paris.

Following the First World War, the quest for fun fuelled the development of haute couture. Between 1914 and 1929, the number of couture houses in Paris jumped from around 20 to 200. Fashion stepped into modernity. Women, who had replaced men in industry while they were fighting at the front, were disinclined to go back to more formal attire – they now needed a wardrobe for the active individuals they had become. Of course, not all women could afford couture, but imitations were common at a time when fashion houses did not offer ready-to-wear.

Between the wars, Paris became the capital of fashion, but the Second World War took its toll on this burgeoning status. While impoverished Europe was no longer able to

Grace Jones, depicted by Jean-Paul Goude, on the cover of 1981's
Nightclubbing. Jones was a fixture of the Paris scene in the 70s and 80s.

provide Americans with bespoke garments, these countries
developed their own industry, focused on ready-to-wear.
Playing on its assets, France fought back with its expertise in
couture. In the fifties, Christian Dior's ultra-feminine lines
became the "New Look". French couturiers' creations were
worn by famous actresses , every other cover of *American
Vogue* mentioned "Paris" and the city became the backdrop
to whimsical movies such as *An American in Paris* (1951).
Hollywood reinforced Paris's position as the fashion capital.

Since Coco Chanel's revolution in the twenties, French style
had been associated with chic simplicity, but in the sixties,
liberated young people aspired to break away from their
parents' demure styles. All eyes were on Swinging London,
but Paris was ready to keep up. A coterie of new designers

emerged, choosing luxe ready-to-wear over couture. André Courrèges and Paco Rabanne nailed it when it came to the futuristic fashion the younger crowd were longing for. The new Parisian icons were English – Jane Birkin and Loulou de la Falaise brought some of London's freedom in their suitcases, forging the modern Parisian silhouette, a more laid-back take on the city's timeless elegance. With his alluring silhouettes, mixing masculine and feminine, Yves Saint Laurent was fast becoming the ultimate Parisian designer.

Since then, the style of "La Parisienne" has gently evolved along with the new trends. Wider and shinier in the eighties, more sporty and minimal in the nineties. Loud international Y2K trends never made it through the Parisian elite's polished taste, who preferred the retro *Amélie* vibes also trending. That doesn't mean they were not present in Paris, but they were not considered "Parisian", which confirms "Paris style" as being an aesthetic rather than a city.

Indeed, the city of Paris is a formidable tool in itself when it comes to promoting its own style. Joining the Fashion Week calendar in 1973, Paris Fashion Week soon became the most sought-after gig, with its dramatic shows located in famous historical landmarks. French brands max out the image of their beloved city, featuring it in the background of much of their clothing and perfume advertising.

Through 2000–2010, "La Parisienne" experienced a comeback with books dedicated to her effortless style and Instagrammers building their fame on this dreamy lifestyle. In the 2020s, the concept is still a powerful marketing argument, although critiqued by books such as *Je ne suis pas Parisienne*, published in 2019 by French journalist Alice Pfeiffer.

"Parisienne" or not, there is something in the style of France's capital that makes it unique.

French singer, model and actress Vanessa Paradis wears a
heart pendant choker and black sheer top, 1992.

chapter 1

INSiDE
PARiSiAN
STYLE

PERFUME

Chanel N°5, J'adore by Dior, Angel by Thierry Mugler ... the world's most popular fragrances were created by Parisian fashion brands.

Perfume entered the French elite's lifestyle after the Black Death ingrained a fear of water, believed to carry diseases which scents repelled. Aristocrats used such generous amounts of perfume that Versailles was nicknamed "the perfumed court". Most fragrances were produced in Grasse, in the South of France, nowadays known as the capital of fragrance.

Until the twentieth century, perfumes were produced by specialized companies such as Guerlain, once supplier to the Emperor. Chanel was the first couture house to commercialize a perfume under the designer's own signature. In 1920, Coco Chanel asked *nez* (perfume nose) Ernest Beaux to create "a women's perfume that smells like a woman". It was a true designer perfume, befitting the unique spirit of the brand. Beaux came back with five numbered extracts. Coco chose number five, which contained 80 ingredients, including aldéhyde, a synthetic component. When asked what to name it, Chanel replied, "I release my collection May 5th, the fifth month of the year. Let's keep the number, it will be good luck."

Following the Second World War, every French couture house was to launch their own *jus* (juice) – the term used by professionals for the perfume's liquid. In 1947, Christian Dior's very first collection was launched with the iconic Miss Dior fragrance, a scent true to the designer's passion for flowers – "A perfume is a dress's finishing touch," declared the couturier.

Inside Parisian Style

Chanel No. 5 perfume bottle advert, 1927.

A nautical-themed Jean Paul Gaultier perfume advert from the 1990s, featuring mermaids, sailors and a sinking Eiffel Tower.

Over the years, sales volumes of perfume increased with the power of marketing. First, bottles became more elaborate, embodying the spirit of the brand. Advertisements evolved from simple illustrations to professional photographs and then to film footage. The House of Chanel was one of the first to use ambassadors to represent its perfumes. Coco Chanel initially did the job herself, posing in a 1937 Chanel N°5 campaign before hiring a series of actresses and models. French houses have since hired celebrities like Catherine Deneuve, Carole Bouquet, Sophie Marceau and Vanessa Paradis before turning to internationally famous celebrities.

Brands use the Paris dream factor. In 1928, Bourjois launched Soir de Paris (Evening in Paris) with top notes of violet, apricot, peach and bergamot. The illustrative advertisement showed a couple at night, passing by some of Paris's most famous monuments such as the Arc de Triomphe, the Fontaines de la Concorde and the Eiffel Tower (on later ads, obviously). The year 1935 heralded the arrival of Lancôme – so-named to sound like "Vendôme". In 1983, Yves Saint Laurent created Paris, a violet-based perfume. The 1992 ad featured a couple kissing between the Eiffel Tower and a helicopter. The perfumes Parisienne and Mon Paris would later be released by the brand.

The marketing force of couture houses overpowered most *parfumeurs*, which slowly disappeared. Tired of the "all in the marketing" approach, a French niche perfume scene emerged, with brands such as Annick Goutal and Frédéric Malle valuing perfume-making expertise, creativity and quality ingredients.

Since its glorious Renaissance days, France hasn't lost its touch, with fragrance one of its key exports. The French love of scent continues, with most Françaises regularly using it.

The unique know-how of the French lingerie industry forged the local taste for sophisticated undergarments, and France eventually became famous worldwide for its underwear.

In the late 1800s, corsets were the norm. Aiming to free women by liberating their bodies, the skilled worker Herminie Cadolle invented "*le bien-être*" (the well-being) – a "*corselet-gorge*". In other words, a corset split in two parts for more ease of movement, the upper part being the brassière, as we know it nowadays. It took around 30 years until the "*soutien-gorge*" became mainstream.

The quality of French lingerie relies on skilled workers' *corseterie* expertise along with the use of high-quality home-sourced fabrics such as *dentelle* (lace) or silk.

As luxury products, bras were once stored in the drawers of fancy boutiques. In the sixties, Etam created a series of affordable cotton underwear presented on hangers, allowing better access for clients. Lingerie was mostly available in neutral shades until the sisters Loumia and Shama Hiridjee decided to sell fun fashionable underwear in their Paris boutique. They named their brand Princesse Tam Tam based on the 1935 movie starring Josephine Baker. Witty and affordable, it is a modern success story.

Lingerie remains a thriving industry in France. Keen purchasers of fancy sets, the French are the foremost buyers of underwear in Europe, according to the Institut Français de la Mode.

Lella, Bretagne (Brittany) from *Portfolio* by Édouard Boubat, 1948.

Inside Parisian Style

LES GRANDS MAGASINS

When shopping in Paris, the decor is as important as the purchases!

In the mid-1800s, women purchased items for making clothes such as fabrics and haberdashery from small specialized boutiques. These goods were stored in the back of shops and clients requested what they needed from the *vendeuse* (salesperson). In 1852, husband-and-wife entrepreneurs Aristide and Marguerite Boucicaut turned Au Bon Marché, a Rive Gauche novelty store, into a larger shop dedicated to women's shopping. For the first time, products were displayed so clients could touch them. Prices were fixed (not subject to bargaining as in the smaller shops) and were the lowest in town, thanks to the Boucicauts' preference for mass buying ("*Bon marché*" means cheap).

To offer Parisians a sumptuous setting for their shopping, the Boucicauts hired the civil engineer Gustave Eiffel and architect Louis-Charles Boileau. In 1869, the store was a well-lit glass palace, as described by the writer Émile Zola in *Au Bonheur des Dames* (The Ladies' Delight), a book inspired by the story of Au Bon Marché.

Galvanized by the success of Au Bon Marché, more *grands magasins* were opened on the other side of the Seine: Le Printemps (1865), La Samaritaine (1870) and Galeries Lafayette (1893).

Inside Parisian Style

BAINS DE MER
VILLES D'EAUX

AU BON MARCHÉ
MAISON A. BOUCICAUT. PARIS

Au Bon Marché advert, illustration by René Vincent (1879–1936), Paris.

In the twenty-first century, *grands magasins* are still a must-visit when in Paris. Bon Marché exhibits gigantic artworks, Galeries Lafayette has a rooftop skating rink in winter, Printemps restaurant with its view of the Eiffel tower is not to be missed and the animated Christmas windows are a great favourite.

Inside Parisian Style

s a n d r o

P A R I S

HiGH STREET FASHiON

Grand couturiers may have been a major influence in French fashion, yet the vast majority of Parisiennes have never been able to afford to buy from Dior. Before the fifties, most clothes were made to measure. The richest could afford *"les grands couturiers"*, the middle classes would have dresses assembled by the local seamstress and the lower classes would make their own clothes or thrift.

After the Second World War, France was no longer the first port of call for international fashion, due to a shortage of fabrics. Meanwhile, in the US, Ford production techniques were applied to clothing and a sizing system implemented to create ready-to-wear clothes. Inspired by the US, Weill was the first manufacturer to transform into a brand (a *"griffe"*, meaning signature). To that end, the company hired entrepreneur and advertising magnate Marcel Bleustein-Blanchet, who created the tagline *"un vêtement Weill vous va"* (a Weill garment suits you). From 1948, journalists referred to Weill as a *"prêt-à-porter"* maker (literally translated from the English "ready-to-wear").

In 1952, *ELLE* magazine published an edition about *"prêt-à-porter"* ("Would You Like to Find Your Dresses Already Made?"), shortly followed by *Vogue*. Then, in 1957, a dedicated fair was launched, yet commercial success was modest – old habits were deeply rooted. It took a cultural revolution to really shake the system. Before 1968, youthful fashion was not

Model Edie Campbell in a Sandro Paris advert, 2014.

Inside Parisian Style

Day dress and low-slung belt by Yves Saint Laurent Rive Gauche
worn in front of a sculpture by Niki de Saint Phalle.

really a thing. But then, the new generation of baby boomers aspired to dress differently from their parents, and sewing was a chore that women no longer wanted to do. Affordable *prêt-à porter* brands like Dorothée Bis, NAF NAF and Promod marketed towards young people emerged in the sixties and seventies. Rather than simply reproducing the latest couture trends, they hired stylists or trend consulting agencies to design their collections. Upcoming high-end brands such as Sonia Rykiel and agnès b. deliberately opted for *prêt-à-porter*, and in a bid to attract younger customers, couturiers also started their own ready-to-wear lines. With his Rive Gauche boutique, Yves Saint Laurent was the pioneer. The new generation of couturiers such as Thierry Mugler and Claude Montana launched both lines simultaneously.

In the eighties, market demand accelerated. To supply the latest trends to their young clientele, brands based in the Parisian manufacturing neighbourhood Le Sentier had the idea of customizing their clothes on the spot – a trick that made NAF NAF a phenomenal success with their jumpsuits in 1983. In 1986, the company opened stores across France, promoting them with a memorable slogan: "Who's Afraid of the Big Mean Look?"

The arrival of foreign fast-fashion brands Zara and H&M in the nineties proved a hit with Parisians, who loved to augment their wardrobes with fun, cheap pieces. Meanwhile, some affordable French chains competed by positioning themselves as teen brands like Jennyfer and Pimkie or emphasizing their Frenchness – for example, Promod and Etam. Since 2004, H&M has collaborated with French designers to create capsule collections (Karl Lagerfeld, Sonia Rykiel, Isabel Marant, etc.), making "luxury" accessible to everyone in the process.

Inside Parisian Style

Unable to compete with Zara's collection renewal pace, some of the Le Sentier brands went upmarket. In 1998, Judith Milgrom parted ways with her sister Evelyn Chétrite (with whom she founded Sandro) to launch her own brand, Maje. Allies rather than competitors, the pair have a similar positioning: selling high-fashion clothes in sophisticated boutiques for mid-range prices. Maje is more girly, Sandro more rock. Opened in 2004, in le Marais, the first Sandro boutique lifted the neighbourhood's fashion appeal and soon became *the* place to shop. With these smaller boutiques, such brands recreate the intimacy that was lost with megastores.

Many French brands fall into the mid-range category with different style identities and audiences – for example, classic Comptoir des Cotonniers or APC, bohemian chic Gerard Darel and Pablo, sexy rock Iro, and Marant-esque ba&sh. Over the years, those high-end chains have taken over the *centre-villes* (city centres) of many French cities. Previously, "*multimarques*", multi-brand boutiques, were the most common. Their style and selection are unique, based on the owner's personality, who develops close bonds with his clients. In Paris, concept stores made this endangered species fashionable again, with Colette, the epitome of the hype, opening in 2000. In 2022, boho concept stores Merci and Centre Commercial are thriving, with high-end selections.

In the 2010s, new mid-range brands launched online. Retro French Sézane was established in 2013 and a store opened in Paris in 2016. Similarly, colourful Make My Lemonade was created in 2015 by blogger and entrepreneur Lisa Gachet, with the first store opening in 2018, and superstar influencer Jeanne Damas's cult brand Rouje. However, stylish Parisians know the more unique garments will always be found in vintage stores ...

French model Julia Frauche at the Isabel Marant
for H&M collection in Paris in 2013.

VINTAGE

Parisians love being unique, and what's more unique than something thrifted?

Before the Industrial Revolution, clothes were expensive and wearing second-hand or thrifted clothes was common for poorer people. Clothes were either gifted as charity by the rich or acquired from specialized merchants, "*chiffoniers*", who sold old garments collected on the pavement. To improve the environment of the Haussmannian city, *chiffoniers* were no longer permitted to sell on the streets and French lawyer and diplomat Eugène Poubelle introduced waste containers in 1880, so removing their source of material.

To regulate the sale of second-hand garments, a wooden market was built in the city of Paris – in the heart of le Marais, Le Carreau du Temple – in 1808. It was divided into four areas, with Le Palais-Royal specializing in fashion pieces. Banished from town, other merchants also established themselves just outside the city limits in Saint-Ouen. At first an informal gathering, it was officially turned into a market in 1885 and became a steady business as merchants built tiny houses. In the twenties, "*le marché au puces*" (the flea market) was a popular place for a Sunday stroll, where cheap purchases could be made while listening to jazz music and eating out. From 1946 to 1991, 12 other markets were built, making Les Puces de Saint-Ouen one of the biggest antique and thrift markets in the world. In 2022, it is a fashionable

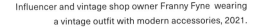

Influencer and vintage shop owner Franny Fyne wearing a vintage outfit with modern accessories, 2021.

An affordable Parisian market at the Carreau du Temple in Paris, 1956.

area where well-dressed Parisians source a variety of pre-loved garments, from vintage couture to basic thrift.

Another weekend thrifting option is *"vide-greniers"* and *"brocantes"*. At the former, people sell their own clothes while the latter is for professional dealers only. In spring and autumn, these events, located directly in the streets, are packed. They have existed since the early twentieth century when temporary *"foires à la ferraille"* were spotted around the Bastille neighbourhood.

Due to the boom of ready-to-wear collections in the sixties, the number of clothes owned by a single person rose steadily and, from the seventies onwards, consignment stores (*"dépôts-ventes"*) opened for people to make room in their closets while earning a bit of extra cash. Some still exist, like La Marelle, established since 1974 in Galerie Vivienne in the

Inside Parisian Style

2nd arrondissement. In the early 2020s, there are dozens of these places in Paris, each with their own identity, reviving the glorious time of multi-brand stores.

Paris is also blessed with a large number of vintage and thrift stores. The cheapest ones, like Guerrisol and Free'p'star, buy in bulk and sell without sorting. Slightly more expensive thrifts such as Kiliwatch stock only trendy products organized in categories. The popularity of thrift stores waned with the rise of fast fashion, but in recent years environmental concerns and a desire to be unique have made thrifting more popular than ever. The fanciest vintage stores display a carefully curated selection. Their owners are experts who know all about fashion history. Most favour brands, others periods, some a mix; each has their own personality. In Paris, the most celebrated is Didier Ludot – established in Palais Royal since 1975, he sells only couture.

After the 2008 financial crisis, resale websites like French Vestiaire Collective and Lithuanian Vinted became highly popular, democratizing second-hand and making it appealing to fashion lovers. What was once considered to be a buying pattern for those in need became gentrified. Now even wealthy people do not shy away from buying at charity or bulk thrifts. Many French influencers wear vintage. As early as 2008, Betty Autier blogged about the cool clothes she found at Guerrisol for a few euros. Since 2017, influencer Sophie Fontanel has reported on her flea market excursions and is also an ambassador for leboncoin (an online garage sale). In Paris, there is a whole clique of vintage influencers, including chic Frannfyne and eccentric Zoehtq (who documents her outfit creation process on TikTok). These vintage influencers assemble clothes from different eras to compose contemporary outfits. For less wealthy consumers, who could only dream of luxury items, vintage is a way to buy quality at a more reasonable price.

VOGUE AND ELLE

Before the rise of social media, printed magazines were the main source of inspirational fashion images. Printed magazines for a female audience have been around since the late 1800s in France. *La Mode Illustrée* (founded 1860) and *Le Petit Écho de la Mode* (1880) were designed to help women in various aspects of their daily life. They contained advice on how to wear the trends and how to dress the family, along with sewing patterns.

Launched in 1920, the French edition of *Vogue* was more inspirational than practical. Features were penned by acknowledged writers and columnists while illustrations were produced by up-and-coming artists. Soon, talented photographers like Lee Miller and Horst were hired. With its elegant layout, the magazine appealed to the bourgeoisie.

In 1945, journalist Hélène Gordon-Lazareff created *ELLE*. The magazine contained both frivolous and serious features, covering topics like the women's fight for abortion along with reports on the latest fashions. A mix of genre is still present in 2022 although the magazine's sometimes conservative take on feminist topics is often critiqued.

In 1968, *Le Vogue Français* became *Vogue Paris*, with "Paris" written inside the "O". According to Carine Roitfeld, editor-in-chief from 2001–11, "*Vogue Paris* is edgier and has more influence on designers [than the original *Vogue*], it has that French, often provocative spirit" (*Le Monde*, 2010). After the French cultural revolution, *Vogue Paris* became quite daring,

Art deco-style on the cover of *Vogue France*, August 1929.

releasing alluring editorials by groundbreaking artist Guy
Bourdin and the iconic photographer Helmut Newton. With
her sexy, chic style, Roitfeld is a style icon herself and paved
the way for her successor, the discreet Emmanuelle Alt, whose
effortless allure became a favourite of blogging era street-style
photographers.

In France, as in other Western countries, women's magazines
established the prejudiced idea that the fashionable woman
should be white, thin and young. In 1966, editor-in-chief
Edmonde Charles-Roux left her position at *Vogue* because she
was not allowed to choose a woman of colour for the cover.
The first Black model to make the cover would be Naomi
Campbell, some 22 years later. In 2022, covers featuring non-
white models are still a rarity and the same can be said of
plus-size models and older women.

In 2021, Anna Wintour appointed 32-year-old Eugénie
Trochu as head of editorial content for *Vogue Paris*, which
she immediately rebranded *Vogue France*. Not Parisian-
born herself, this young woman aims to make *Vogue* more
inclusive. For her first cover, she chose the Black rapper Aya
Nakamura: "I want to change the image of French women
so that everyone can identify, Aya Nakamura is very popular,
here [...] She is chic while remaining herself."

Struggling with new generations who increasingly turn
to digital rather than paper, magazines adapt their
communication and contents. Trochu shares her daily work
and private life on social media. Meanwhile, the online
version of *ELLE* shares fun fashion content and advice that
had, in recent years, been replaced by less relatable high
fashion in the print edition.

Then-editor-in-chief of *Vogue Paris* Carine Roitfeld attends the 2010
Fair Game Cocktail Party hosted by Giorgio Armani in Cannes, France.

Inside Parisian Style

Parisian influencers benefit from the city's beautiful settings and the aura of "la Parisienne".

Since the early noughties, those with a passion for style have shared their outfits and fashion thoughts online. With their witty talk and stylish illustrations, Betty Autier and Garance Doré fast became favourites. The two Parisiennes, who translated their posts into English, soon reached an international audience.

In 2009, Garance Doré published a post titled "La Femme Française" in which she answered one of her American readers who asked how to add a French touch to her wardrobe. In her mischievous way, Doré pretended to debunk the myths while acknowledging them (after listing the many stripes in her wardrobe: "Non. Non, I don't think we can conclude that the French woman (esp. someone named Garance Doré) wears one too many stripes. ;-).")

Others used emerging social media to document their daily outfits. Under the name "Crevette Liloo", Jeanne Damas became a teenage micro celebrity on the French platform skyblog, before garnering over 1.5 million followers on her Insta, which is packed with Parisian style inspiration.

Over time, Insta has diversified the sources we look to for inspiration, with different ages, sizes and skin tones being represented – for example by fifty-something ex-journalist Sophie Fontanel, sophisticated plus-size influencer

Designer and model Jeanne Damas in jeans and a leather jacket outside the Valentino show during Paris Fashion Week, March 2020.

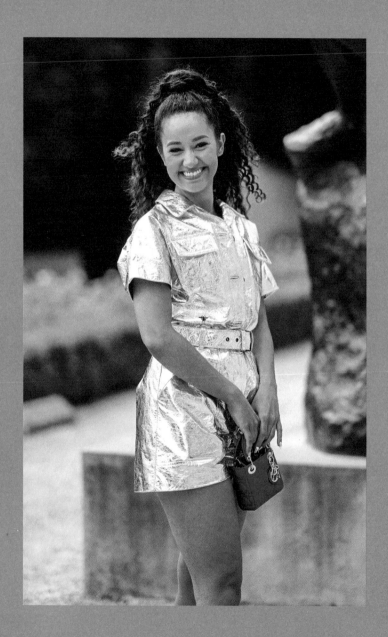

Lalaa Misaki and Black beauty blogger Fatou N'diaye aka Blackbeautybag.

45

Léna Mahfouf, aka Léna Situations, was the most powerful influencer in the world in 2021 – going from posting on YouTube about her daily life since 2017 to being a Dior ambassador and making videos for *Vogue*. She is the sweetheart of the French fashion establishment.

"La Parisienne of Insta reinvents the codes of French style for a new generation."

Sporting Breton stripes, sexy denim, basket bags, vintage florals and retro knits, La Parisienne of Insta reinvents the codes of French style for a new generation. Many influencers capitalize on Paris's fashion appeal to build their fame. French icons Jeanne Damas and Anne-Laure Mais have attracted millions of followers by sharing their effortlessly cool outfits photographed on the streets of Paris, as well as their effortlessly chic apartments. The two have founded successful clothing lines around their fame (Rouje and Musier now have legions of fans around the world). It's not easy to emerge in a world of plenty but with millions of entries, hashtags frenchgirl and frenchstyle are a social media hit. To be noticed, newcomers love clichés: surrounded by Haussmannian buildings, hanging out in cafés and eating croissants, they often pay a visit to the Eiffel Tower too. In their videos, these Jane Birkin-inspired muses capture an idealized Parisian life, all to a background of French music from the sixties.

Inside Parisian Style

YouTuber Léna Mahfouf (known as Léna Situations) wears a statement silver playsuit outside the Dior show, Paris Fashion Week, July 2021.

CULTURE IS FASHIONABLE

In the Parisian's somewhat cliquish society, being cultured is regarded as hotter than logos.

In the seventeenth century, wit and education were considered attractive traits in women. Of his 25 years junior wife, the poet Paul Scarron said, "She comes with two mischievous eyes, a pair of beautiful hands and lots of wit." Then in the nineteenth century, literary salons were the place to be seen for the city's most influential women, but let's not be fooled, it was still a world of men.

In Nouvelle Vague movies, culture plays a big part in a character's sex appeal. They are seen reading, quoting verse, painting ... Women especially are pictured reading books – Anna Karina in Jean-Luc Godard's *Alphaville* (1965), Brigitte Bardot taking a bath in *Le Mépris* (1963) and Haydée Politoff in Eric Rohmer's *La Collectionneuse* (1967). In the eighties, Sophie Marceau reads Zola's *L'Assommoir* while sporting big glasses in *L'étudiante* (1988) and in the 2007 movie *Les Chansons d'Amour*, the three main characters read together in bed as a ménage à trois, mimicking an iconic scene from *Domicile Conjugal* (1970) by François Truffaut.

French "It" girls and brands love to replicate this trope. On Instagram, Jeanne Damas poses with André Breton's book *Nadja* covering half her face, Lou Doillon sings in front of her book wall, Rouje (Jeanne Damas's brand) photographs

Inside Parisian Style

Two models standing outside a Parisian bookshop wearing tweed suits from Pierre Balmain's Autumn/Winter 1953 collection.

girls holding books in front of the Quais de Seine bouquinistes, while lingerie brand Ysé models pose in front of bookshelves. Brands also use literature as an opportunity to communicate to their luxury clients. Elegant Rive Gauche store Le Bon Marché invites writers Sophie Fontanel and Morgane Ortin, always impeccably dressed, to discuss their own books. Then in 2021, Chanel launched the podcast "Les Rendez-vous Littéraires de la rue Cambon", an intimate talk with women authors.

Going to the museum is another romanticized part of Paris cultural life. In the Nouvelle Vague movie *Bande à part* (1964), Jean-Luc Godard's characters run through the Louvre, a scene replicated as an homage in *The Dreamers* (2003) by Bernardo Bertolucci. When representing life in Paris, American producers never fail to include a museum stop, whether it's Audrey Hepburn walking down the monumental staircase of the Louvre for a fashion shoot in *Funny Face* (1957) or Blair Waldorf meeting a prince (indeed!) at the Musée d'Orsay in the TV series *Gossip Girl*. Parisian museums are among the influencers' favourite settings, with the Louvre and l'Orangerie considered mainstream, while lesser-known museums like the Bourdelle feel somewhat edgier.

Louise Ebel, aka Miss Pandora, is an influencer with a degree in art history and a true passion for culture. When she first started posting, she would take inspiration from famous paintings to create her outfits. More than a decade later, she is a fashion and culture influencer with a 70k community who follow her patrimonial adventures.

To reinforce their anchorage in French culture, luxury brands use Parisian museums as settings. Louis Vuitton has shot advertising and set their show inside the Louvre twice. They also support the arts with the Fondation Louis Vuitton while the Pinault Collection offers a vibrant perspective on contemporary art. Fashion and music have strong bonds as well.

Inside Parisian Style

Models walk in Louis Vuitton's Autumn/Winter
2021/2022 show at the Louvre, Paris Fashion Week.

Inside Parisian Style

Inès de la Fressange engrossed in a book, Paris, 1987.

Chanel Autumn/Winter 2018/19 at the Grand
Palais, bouquinistes in the background.

Brand ambassadors are often singers, like Angèle for Chanel.
In 2019, Hedi Slimane, the creative director of Céline who has
a passion for music, shared a playlist of 20 songs on Spotify.

Fashion plays a key part in French culture, with three museums
in Paris dedicated to it. Musée de la Mode was created in
1954, and since 1977 has been installed in the Palais Galliera.
Musée des Arts Décoratifs (MAD), founded in 1905 to display
collections of industrial arts including textiles, is located in a
wing of the Louvre. And finally, there is the privately owned
Musée Yves Saint Laurent Paris, opened in 2017.

Of course French culture is much more than books and ancient
museums, but internationally, these symbols are known as
semaphores for the sophisticated French intellect.

CIGARETTES

Although far from pretty on the inside, cigarettes have long been seen by fashionable Parisiennes as an elegant accessory – toted by icons such as Coco Chanel, Catherine Deneuve, Jane Birkin and Charlotte Gainsbourg.

In the 1920s liberated *garçonnes* began smoking cigarettes just like men. They used *porte-cigarettes* (cigarette holders), creating a long line that echoed the desired silhouette of the times.

Couturier Yves Saint Laurent's first scandalous creation was his 1966 woman's "Le Smoking". A *smoking* is the French name for tuxedo – they were worn by men in smoking rooms. This debut pre-empted the importance of cigarettes in the brand's aesthetic. In a famous 1975 photo, an androgynous woman smokes a cigarette in a quaint Parisian street wearing the tuxedo.

Kate Moss made a buzz when smoking on the Louis Vuitton runway in 2012. It was a classic move in eighties Chanel shows, where Coco lookalike Inès de la Fressange would play with her cigarettes or cigars on the catwalk.

Cigarettes might have been forbidden in advertising since 1991, but French makeup brands now have models smoking ... lipsticks! They hold them opened, like a cigarette whose fiery end would be the makeup.

Astonishingly, over a quarter of French women still smoke. Although we now know that smoking kills, the iconic image of the smoking Parisienne endures.

Inside Parisian Style

Inès de la Fressange smokes a cigar on the runway in Paris, 1982.

LA TOUR EIFFEL

Both emblems of Paris, fashion and the Eiffel Tower often collide.

The Eiffel Tower is a popular backdrop for fashion shoots. Sometimes up-close, like Erwin Blumenfeld's 1933 photos of the Swedish model Lisa Fonssagrives wearing a skirt floating on the beams of the Tower, or the American supermodel Dovima photographed by Richard Avedon and wearing Dior in 1950. Those pictures inspired the Lady Dior 2009 campaign by Peter Lindbergh, starring actress Marion Cotillard.

The iconic tower is a staple of many perfume ads – as in a drawing in 1959 for Soir de Paris by Bourjois, or, more recently, drawn for Guerlain's La Petite Robe Noire and sparkling in La Vie Est Belle by Lancôme. La Tour Eiffel features in the background of many Dior campaigns and is one of the main subjects in Yves Saint Laurent's Paris-themed perfume line.

For Louis Vuitton, Jacques-Henri Lartigue photographed a mini Eiffel Tower made up of luggage in front of the real tower in 1978. This iconic image was later reproduced in the windows of the luxury brand's Champs-Élysées flagship store in 2012 and printed on accessories such as keychains

Cecile Chevreau as Joan Peterson in *Paid to Kill*, wearing an evening dress by Madeleine de Rauch in front of the Eiffel Tower, 1954.

Inside Parisian Style

and card-holders. The "Dame de Fer" (the Iron Lady and, no, not Margaret!) is one of the stars of the playful campaigns directed by Jean-Paul Goude for Galeries Lafayette. The tower makes for memorable catwalks, whether the real one, sparkling behind models at the Saint Laurent show since 2018, or a replica, beneath which Chanel models walked in 2017.

Sometimes the silhouette of the tower makes its way into collections – a witty choice given that any Eiffel Tower ornament is ridiculed as "tourist behaviour", as seen when Emily (in Paris) is mocked because of the tower-shaped charms on her bag in the 2020 TV comedy-drama. Yet with "*second degré*" (a bit of irony), the print can be worn with panache by those in the know.

In 2018, Balenciaga released a bag laden with Eiffel Tower charms and the following year, a black velvet suit scattered with the tower's silhouette duplicated in rhinestones (later worn by Carine Roitfeld, former editor-in-chief of *Vogue*). The same humorous spirit can be found in the brand's 2021–22 lookbook, where models pose like typical tourists (pinching the tower). In 2000, Jean Paul Gaultier had models walk the runway wearing dresses or tights with enormous Eiffel Tower placed patterns.

Locations with the best views over the Tower, such as rue de l'Université, are now filled from dawn till dusk with amateur and professional photographers alike, seeking the perfect Insta backdrop.

A model wears an Eiffel Tower-print dress, Balenciaga Spring/Summer 2019.

chapter 2

iCONiC DESiGNERS

COCO CHANEL

Elegant simplicity

When looking for a designer to embody the Parisienne's allure, Coco Chanel is the first to come to mind. Translating her love for practicality, simple lines and neutral colours into clothes and accessories, she single-handedly defined the template for the Parisienne's now legendary casual chic.

Amid Belle Époque flounces galore, the young Gabrielle "Coco" Chanel preferred to dress "like a little boy" rather than be corseted in voluminous dresses. Since she couldn't find hats that suited her love of simple designs, she started making her own, and soon encountered great success among her friends, leading her to open her Parisian boutique on rue Cambon in 1910. From there she was unstoppable, soon founding her couture house and following with jewellery, perfume and beauty lines. The Chanel aesthetic became a whole lifestyle.

Coco's personality itself embodies the ideal Parisienne as she exists in most people's imaginations. Independent, witty and unapologetic, she led a nonconformist life as an unmarried career woman.

Coco Chanel demonstrating her signature chic and understated style in 1944, Paris.

Iconic Designers

Chanel's way of conceiving fashion was incredibly modern. She created clothes for women who were subjects rather than objects. Her aim was for her designs to make a woman's personality radiate rather than drown it under layers of fabrics. "If a woman is poorly dressed, you notice the dress. If she is impeccably dressed, you notice her."

Seeing her clothes on the streets was one of her greatest rewards. When asked about it in 1959, she replied: "Creating a style was what I aimed for. There was no style anymore in France. There is a style in a nation when people in the streets are dressed like I do, and I think I achieved this."

Almost a century later, pieces created by Chanel have become staples of French style.

As she declared, "May my legend gain ground – I wish it a long and happy life." She got what she wanted.

Chanel's legacy

- Striped shirts
- The tweed jacket
- A bold use of costume jewellery and shiny ornaments (buttons!)
- The 2.55, a revolutionary bag that could be carried on the shoulder
- Pockets, a defining element of the Parisienne's laid-back posture
- A neutral colour palette with red accents

Iconic Designers

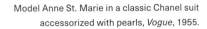

Model Anne St. Marie in a classic Chanel suit accessorized with pearls, *Vogue*, 1955.

ELSA SCHIAPARELLI

Eccentric chic

Parisian fashion is sometimes seen as restrained, yet some of its most iconic designers are known for their eccentric creations. The Italian-born aristocrat Elsa Schiaparelli mesmerized Parisian high society with her artsy designs.

Schiaparelli's tumultuous private life led her to land in Paris in 1922 as a 30-year-old mother and divorcée. While making a modest living from thrifting and retailing, Elsa was daydreaming of Paul Poiret's costly apparel made of sultry fabric and intricate embroideries. At this time the major couturier, who freed women from corsets by creating a fluid silhouette, was already becoming passé. His fragile dresses were not fit for the lifestyles of modern women who were now into Coco Chanel's sporty attire.

A young woman herself, Schiaparelli was interested in activewear, but dissatisfied with the associated styles, which were too simple for her liking. To each problem a solution: she created the now iconic trompe-l'oeil pussy-bow jumper. The immediate success it encountered drove her to create her own couture house.

Iconic Designers

Elsa Schiaparelli wearing a black silk dress with crocheted collar of her own design and a turban, 1940.

"Really good clothes never go out of fashion."
Elsa Schiaparelli, Shocking Life

Blessed with a boundless imagination, she was one of the first designers to create collections based on themes like the circus or the zodiac. Her clothes always had at least one extravagant characteristic to make it memorable: the cut, the colour, the print or the accessories. The emblem of her bold chic was a pink with a hint of magenta so loud it could be spotted from afar. She named it "shocking pink".

Well-connected Schiaparelli was hanging out with "le tout Paris" and artsy crowds. Following the path of her mentor Paul Poiret, who once had painter Dufy design a print for him, she collaborated with several of her artist friends to create museum-worthy pieces of clothing, like the memorable Salvador Dalí lobster-adorned dress. A true artist herself, she always created the most unique designs.

Schiaparelli's legacy

- The art of unique artsy detail
- Bold colours as a statement
- Humour in fashion

Iconic Designers

A red satin, visored evening cap with an elongated peephole for the eye by Schiaparelli, 1949.

CHRISTIAN DIOR

Architectured femininity

The extreme sophistication of Christian Dior's first creations may not be commonly encountered on Parisian streets nowadays, yet the revolutionary couturier instilled a sense of architecture that has imprinted fashion forever.

Born in 1905, Christian Dior was passionate about architecture but his bourgeois father insisted he study at the Paris Institute of Political Studies instead. Seeking a creative career, Christian left and opened an art gallery before trying to make a living as a fashion illustrator. After a bumpy life, he landed the position of "assistant stylist" for Lucien Lelong, at the age of 37. Four years later, he persuaded wealthy investor Marcel Boussac to invest in his own brand. In 1947, Christian Dior couture was born.

His first collection was a resounding success. In opposition to the masculine, minimal lines made prevalent by the necessities of war, Christian Dior created rounded shoulders, a cinched waist and long voluminous skirts: the "Huit" and "Corolle" hyper-feminine silhouettes. "Your dresses have such a new look," said Carmel Snow, editor of *Harper's Bazaar*. With their opulent lining and obscene volume of

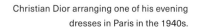

Christian Dior arranging one of his evening dresses in Paris in the 1940s.

fabric, the dresses caused a scandal in impoverished post-war France, before being adopted by Parisiennes looking for glamour and relief following years of deprivation.

Christian Dior's creations were filled with floral colours and prints inspired by his childhood house in Normandy, a location he cherished above all. When asked who the gardener of her blooming garden was, his mother would answer, "Oh, that's my son." Florals have been a code of the House of Dior ever since, used in the perfumes, the colour scheme and the shows' staging.

In the following years the couturier kept reinventing the silhouette's architecture. The "natural line" with softer curves, the "long line" for a lengthier silhouette, the "A line" with wide hips and a less cinched waist, and the unexpected "Y line" with broader shoulders. Ten years after its launch, the couture house was successful worldwide when Christian Dior suddenly passed away, leaving his legacy in the hands of his young assistant: Yves Saint Laurent.

Dior's legacy

- Contemporary glamour
- Floral prints and shades
- The cinched Bar jacket

Iconic Designers

The audience admires one of Christian Dior's creations at his Paris salon, 1950s.

CHLOÉ

Liberated romanticism

Moving in flowy cuts, Chloé "girls" (as the brand describes them) embody the carelessness of the seventies. Nowadays, they are the posh boho girls hanging out between Saint-Germain-des-Prés and the 11th arrondissement.

Wealthy, Egyptian-born Gaby Aghion wanted to break away from the corseted couture of the fifties. She dreamt of soft garments women could "live their life in". For her first collection in 1952, Gaby did not want to go through the long and costly process of made to measure. Instead she chose to create a prêt-à-porter (ready-to-wear) line with luxury quality standards. To achieve this, she hired an haute couture-trained seamstress to create the six designs she had drawn and bought the highest-quality materials herself.

Then, the daring young entrepreneur knocked on the door of couture houses – who were starting to offer a range of ready-to-wear in their boutiques – to sell them her creations. It was an immediate success, which encouraged her to create her brand under the name Chloé (borrowed from her best friend). It was an immediate success.

Iconic Designers

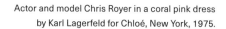

Actor and model Chris Royer in a coral pink dress
by Karl Lagerfeld for Chloé, New York, 1975.

A model wears polka dots by Karl Lagerfeld
for Chloé in Paris for *Vogue*, 1977.

Chloé's DNA is inspired by Gaby's youth in Egypt. The dresses are light and flowy, the soft earthy colour palette reminiscent of the desert's sand and pyramids.

About one her first dresses, Aghion said: "Creating a dress like a T-shirt was avant-garde. This dress encountered a crazy success cause it meant 'I am cool'."

Soon Gaby decided to hire a trained designer to develop her vision. Gifted to see talent in others, she chose young Karl Lagerfeld in 1966, who lifted the house to greater fame.

Until 1985, with Gaby in the background, he developed Chloé's bohemian vibes around flimsy dresses, mixed with boyish styles and a joyful attitude.

Chloé's legacy

- The silk blouse, a Parisian staple
- Accessible luxury
- Boho femininity
- Powdery colour palette
- Natural makeup and floaty hair

Iconic Designers

CÉLINE

Cool bourgeoise

In the seventies and eighties, the models in the advertisements for Céline look like the cool mothers and daughters of Paris's poshest arrondissement. Their mood is so timelessly Parisian, the silhouettes could be worn today.

Céline Vipiana and her husband Roger were initially running a children's shoe business that was "the place to buy" for rich Parisian moms. An entrepreneur at heart, Céline had the idea of starting a shoe line for those wealthy women. Her first success was a pair of comfy loafers which she embellished with a bronze buckle.

In 1967, she designed her first clothing collection, baptized "sportswear couture". That original title remains the guideline for Céline's DNA. Clothes from the house are meant to be both practical and classy. The shapes are ample and fluid for movement, yet structured for chic. Among her favourites are the trench coat, the skirt and shirt combo and culottes. The colour palette is understated with a dominance of neutrals such as beige, brown or grey.

Céline's legacy

- *Les jupes culottes* (culottes, or divided skirts), which are both chic and practical
- Loafers as a staple
- Neutral tartan as a staple

Iconic Designers

A sporty look from the House of Céline shown in Paris, 1979.

YVES SAINT LAURENT

Daring allure

In 1966, Yves Saint Laurent caused a scandal with a tuxedo. Never had an item of menswear been shown in a collection for women. Yves Saint Laurent's fashion DNA is contained in this suit, a combination of couture perfection, power and scandal. It's an irreverence that speaks to the Parisienne's rebel heart.

Freshly arrived from Oran, the shy, 19-year-old Yves Mathieu Saint Laurent was hired by Christian Dior and soon became his first assistant. Two years later, after the death of his mentor, he was appointed head of the house.

With the help of businessman Pierre Bergé (with whom he was also romantically involved), he launched his own couture house. From his debut collection he reinvented masculine wardrobe staples, transforming them into womenswear. First the trench coat and the pea coat in 1962, followed by the shocking tuxedo in 1966, the safari jacket in 1967, and the jumpsuit in 1968.

"Nothing is more beautiful than a naked body," said Yves Saint Laurent, who would later himself pose unclothed for

Yves Saint Laurent poses with muses Loulou de la Falaise (right) and Betty Catroux (left), 1969.

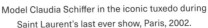

Model Claudia Schiffer in the iconic tuxedo during
Saint Laurent's last ever show, Paris, 2002.

photographer Jean-Loup Sieff. True to this statement, in 1966 he created transparent clothes, through which the breasts showed – a look embodying the sexual revolution that was taking place.

Yves Saint Laurent is famous for his dominant use of black. "Black is my favorite colour – I think that without black there is no line." Influenced by North Africa, he also made a bold use of intense shades and innovated by creating sharp colour clashes across the spectrum. The memorable 1965 Mondrian dress incorporates all those features.

Couture is extremely expensive. For his clothes to be accessible to more women, the Yves Saint Laurent Rive Gauche ready-to-wear line was launched in 1966. "I was bored creating dresses for jaded billionaires," said Saint Laurent. In 1968, he was the first to open a ready-to-wear boutique under his own name – an immediate success that made his brand ubiquitous among Parisiennes. As writer Marguerite Duras said, "Saint Laurent women have been liberated from the harems, castles and suburbs. They run free on the street, the métro, the Prisunic [supermarket] and the stock market".

Yves Saint Laurent aimed to empower women through style. As he said: "Fashion fades, style is forever" – and as Pierre Bergé said: "Chanel gave women freedom. Saint Laurent gave them power."

Saint Laurent's legacy

- Women in trousers
- Intense colours for daytime
- See-through fabrics

Iconic Designers

SONIA RYKIEL

Mischievous feminist

On Sonia Rykiel's runways, models smile, skip and blow kisses – as free as the red-headed designer who created their colourful stretchy jumpers and frilly dresses.

In the sixties, Sonia Rykiel was frustrated that she was unable to find form-hugging knitwear. She asked an Italian wool manufacturer to produce what she had in mind, asking for the knit to be as thin as possible. The sample had to be remade seven times before she was content.

A supporter of the revolutionary events of May 1968, Sonia Rykiel created clothes that restricted movement as little as possible while also being revealing. Here was a way to empower women as independent beings, ready to seduce rather than be seduced.

Sonia Rykiel placed self-expression above fashion, giving women licence to be their own stylists.

Sonia Rykiel's legacy

- Body-hugging knits
- Fun with stripes
- Rhinestones for daytime

Iconic Designers

Models wear eclectic Sonia Rykiel Spring/Summer 2010 creations.

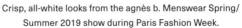

Crisp, all-white looks from the agnès b. Menswear Spring/
Summer 2019 show during Paris Fashion Week.

AGNÈS B.

Charismatic nonchalance

agnès b. created her most iconic piece in 1979: the snap cardigan, with popper closure, that you can open in a flash. This alluring and practical staple encapsulates her style.

agnès b. stepped into the fashion game in 1973 with a down-to-earth approach and youthful minimalist style that stood out in an era of sophistication. Beside the press-on cardigan, the marinière, white shirt and long-sleeved jumpsuit are emblematic of her cool gamine attitude. agnès b. seeks inspiration in workwear for her designs and fabrics. She mostly uses cotton in all its forms alongside high-quality synthetics.

Active in the underground scene, agnès b. sells her clothes in a boutique that is also an art gallery, collaborates with artists for her prints and sponsors an art programme.

"I don't like fashion, I like clothes," she states, standing against the ever-faster renewal of trends.

agnès b.'s legacy

- Street style as a legitimate fashion influence
- The workwear jumpsuit as a daywear staple
- The snap cardigan you can open in a flash
  (not meant to flash people, though)

Iconic Designers

JEAN PAUL GAULTIER

Fun couture

The Parisienne was an endless source of inspiration for Jean Paul Gaultier, who twisted clichés to turn them into couture masterpieces.

At the start of his career, Jean Paul Gaultier worked for couturier Pierre Cardin by day and spent his nights at nightclub Le Palace. The two activities later proved equally formative.

His 1976 self-produced debut collection was messy, according to the designer himself, yet set the base of what would define his joyfully eclectic style, featuring an iconic biker jacket paired with a tutu. Thanks to an investor's financial support, Gaultier was able to develop accomplished collections. Along with the new generation of *créateurs*, he presented them in spectacularly festive fashion shows.

Gaultier's inspirations are manifold. A 1982 Fassbender movie with sexy sailors started his obsession for stripes, and his grandmother's corset was the source of Madonna's cone-breasted satin costume. He is fascinated by pop, rock and underground cultures as well as historical costumes.

Paris is a recurrent theme in his creations. As quoted on the

Iconic Designers

Madonna wearing a Jean Paul Gaultier conical bra corset on her Blond Ambition World Tour, Netherlands, 1990.

Beth Ditto and Jean Paul Gaultier walk the runway at his
Spring/Summer 2011 show during Paris Fashion Week.

brand's website, Gaultier celebrates the "outrageous liberty of the city of lights", "the bad girls, the wild bourgeoises, the cheeky kids, the androgynous creatures and the night queens", never afraid of reinterpreting clichés with cancan-inspired dresses and Eiffel Tower-printed tights. Gaultier has twisted the iconic Parisian trench, a classic since Saint Laurent, in every way possible. He even designed costumes for venerable accordionist Yvette Horner, such as a sparkly flounced dress in the colours of the French Tricolore, and created a "pain couture" exhibit featuring outfits made from baguettes.

Gaultier, who believes that clothes shouldn't be gendered, wears skirts, and dresses women with sailor hats and suspenders. In his perfume advertisements, traditional roles are blurred with toy boys and strong women.

Contrary to the usual snobbery of the fashion elite, Gaultier loves mainstream culture and misfits. Many unusual muses have walked for him: the burlesque dancer Dita Von Teese, the plus-size singer Beth Ditto, French reality TV star Loana and the Eurovision winner and drag queen Conchita Wurst. With his forever bleached hair and marinière, the designer is a pop icon himself.

Thanks to Gaultier and other star designers of the eighties, fashion became fun.

Jean Paul Gaultier's legacy

- Gender-blurring
- Fashion as part of pop culture
- Underwear as outerwear
- French fashion clichés

Iconic Designers

ISABEL MARANT

Urban bohemian

"There isn't a day I don't see a girl wearing my clothes in the streets," observes Isabel Marant (speaking to *Le Monde* in 2019). It's the best reward for a woman who created a cool everyday fashion repertoire. Boho, rock and sexy, Isabel Marant designs clothes she would like to wear herself.

> ## "I want my clothes to be perfect, easy-perfect"
> ### *Isabel Marant*

Marant, who grew up surrounded by stylish people, always preferred cool over sophistication. Shortly after high school, the visionary, environmentally conscious designer created an upcycling brand. She then studied fashion at Studio Berçot and worked for a few years in the industry before launching her eponymous brand in 1995. The presentation of her first collection in a squat using her friends as models was a hit. In 1998, her first boutique in the boho 11th arrondissement was packed with trendy Parisiennes from day one.

Her style is laid-back, inspired by her everyday urban Parisian life and her travels around the world. She mixes

Isabel Marant accepts her applause at the end of her Spring/Summer 2014 show in Paris.

Iconic Designers

boho and sportswear, masculine and girly, romanticism with rock, pairing flowy blouses with biker jackets, frilly miniskirts with platform sneakers, or floral dresses with cowboy boots. *The New Yorker* called her "the woman who defined Parisian cool".

The designer favours natural fabrics like cotton, silk, linen, wool or leather in earthy and subdued shades. When she goes for Barbie pink, inspired by Californian surf culture, the fabric is washed off to lessen its brightness. At Isabel Marant clothes never look "too new".

Marant herself is a natural, sporting her grey hair and no-makeup look everywhere. She creates clothes for women like herself. As she explained to the *Daily Telegraph*, "There's not so many brands you can dress up in every day, for when you have to work, you don't have a driver, when you have to run, bring your kids to school, look good at the office and just after go to dinner with friends. I mean, that's our life."

Isabel Marant's legacy

- Clothes with a patina
- The boho, rock, sporty urban Parisienne
- Sexy cool

Iconic Designers

A model wears head-to-toe earth tones in the Isabel Marant Autumn/Winter 2014/2015 show during Paris Fashion Week.

KARL LAGERFELD

Master of codes

During his 36 years as the creative director of Chanel, Karl Lagerfeld raised the heritage profile of Coco to worldwide brand recognition.

In 1983, Chanel was an ageing house when its owners, the Wertheimer brothers, offered Karl Lagerfeld a role as its new couture and ready-to-wear director. The 49-year-old designer was then successfully freelancing for many renowned houses, including Chloé and Fendi. "Do whatever you want," the Wertheimers told him. "Write that down in the contract," Lagerfeld replied.

A living fashion encyclopaedia, Karl Lagerfeld gave Coco Chanel's iconic creations an up-to-date twist. He shortened the tweed jacket and styled it with jeans. Transformed the camellia brooch into plastic. Exaggerated Coco's love for costume jewellery. Added pop colours. He even shortened the skirts. "I guess she would have ... hated my work," said Lagerfeld. "At the end she hated miniskirts. When you start to disagree with the fashion of a time, you have a problem."

He turned the logo into something fun and chic, inserting it everywhere, starting by replacing the simple 2.55 bag's lock with a double C.

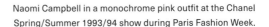

Naomi Campbell in a monochrome pink outfit at the Chanel Spring/Summer 1993/94 show during Paris Fashion Week.

Karl Lagerfeld wearing his iconic sunglasses on the runway at
Chanel Autumn/Winter 2011/2012 during Paris Fashion Week.

To create modern Chanel couture, he relied on the know-how
of the in-house skilled workers, who praised his expertise.
Craft is very important for the House of Chanel which, under
his leadership, absorbed specialized (and historic) workshops
such as the embroiderer Lesage and the plumassier Lemarié
to keep their knowledge alive.

Beside being an excellent designer, Lagerfeld was a master
of marketing and communication. His most unexpected
marketing ploy was to turn himself into a brand. In the
early noughties he slimmed down in order to "fit into Hedi
Slimane's fitted Dior suits". His silhouette became instantly

identifiable: sharp, black and white, with high collars, plenty of rings, black glasses, his sleek white hair tied in a low ponytail.

In 2004, he was the first high fashion designer to create a capsule collection for H&M. The launch was a triumph, all the pieces being sold within minutes in all the fashion capitals.

He transformed Chanel's shows into memorable performances. Firstly, by letting Inès de la Fressange act however she wanted, smoking a cigar on stage or winking mischievously, and then by hiring the decade's most fabulous supermodels such as Claudia Schiffer or Kate Moss. Finally, from 2005 on, he placed the catwalk in the monumental Grand Palais to create grandiose settings, meant to be shared all over social media. Each was more impressive than the next: Parisian rooftops, a vintage brasserie, Deauville's beach (sand and waves included) and even a Chanel rocket!

The revamp of Chanel inspired investors to wake up other "belles endormies", fashion houses with a history and a memorable name that were either closed or which had lost their appeal, and turn them into global luxury brands. We have witnessed the comeback of Carven, Vionnet, Schiaparelli, Patou, Paco Rabanne, Courrèges . . . The history of French couture has become a marketing tool.

Karl Lagerfeld did more than just create couture masterpieces: he brought French couture into the digital global era.

Karl Lagerfeld's legacy

- Playful use of logos
- The concept that each fashion house has its own DNA
- The designer as a pop star

Iconic Designers

HEDI SLIMANE

Classy Rock

Whether he designs for Dior Homme, Saint Laurent or Céline, Hedi Slimane creates "du Slimane": a youthful, rock and glam fashion. "I have always pursued the same character, boy or girl, and in doing so I defined an allure and a silhouette," he told *Le Monde* in 2020.

Born in Paris, the son of a seamstress mother, Hedi Slimane started creating his own clothes from the age of 16 because he couldn't find garments suited for his skinny body. After studying at the École du Louvre, he worked as the assistant to fashion consultant Jean-Jacques Picart before being appointed head of Yves Saint Laurent menswear.

In 2000, his career went into overdrive as Dior Homme's first designer. Since the house had not previously offered menswear, Hedi Slimane was free to create on a blank canvas. From Dior's heritage, he took the structured silhouette. The rest was influenced by his own universe. The "skinny allure" referenced the androgynous men with whom he identified like David Bowie or Serge Gainsbourg. The looks were inspired by the music and the cities he loved: London's rock aesthetic or Berlin's streamlined style.

Iconic Designers

A model wears a gold leopard print dress by Hedi Slimane for the Yves Saint Laurent Spring/Summer 2015 show during Paris Fashion Week.

Hedi Slimane in his signature slim tailoring.

Like Christian Dior in his time, Hedi Slimane invented a new look that everyone wanted. Even women bought Dior Homme, true to Slimane's love for gender fluidity.

From 2012 to 2016, for Saint Laurent Femme, he designed the wardrobe of a party girl, travelling through different music genres and eras. And forever young and sexy, whether in nineties grunge, sixties disco or seventies glam. The Saint Laurent heritage was present in the black dominant lines adorned with intense colours, sequins and lamé. "You do not enter a couture house to mimic the one before you . . . neither do you go against what has been done," he told *Le Figaro*.

Fast-forward to 2018, the designer came back to Paris after 10 years in Los Angeles. His first Céline show, inspired by the Parisian nights of his youth, was wildly criticized because he did Slimane instead of doing Céline. From the next show on, he played with Céline's bourgeois code, reinventing a modern cool and posh Parisienne. "At Céline, I needed to find 'a certain idea of France' [...] to focus on forgotten codes before creating new ones, rooted in my own Parisian culture" (*Le Monde*, 2020). As shows go by, the Céline by Slimane woman remains modern, incorporating sportswear and skater codes into her bourgeois French base.

Designing clothes that are classic, never conceptual, Hedi Slimane creates an allure, a wardrobe.

Hedi Slimane's legacy

- Parisian rock attitude
- A signature without a house
- The skinny silhouette

chapter 3

MYTHICAL STAPLES

THE BERET

The beret is such a cliché that wearing one almost feels un-French. It is the American Emily who wears a red beret when in Paris. Yet the French do wear it, but never too seriously.

Ironically, the origins of the beret are far from fancy – though unclear. Either it developed from the hat worn by shepherds in the Pyrenees in the fifteenth century or it was worn by the onion producers of Brittany.

"A rain coat, a beret, voilà tout!"
Coco Chanel

Made of tight-knit sheep's wool, it is warm, solid and water-repellent. A very practical hat, it was soon adopted by soldiers and scholars. Later, it became part of sporting attire for golfers, alpinists, mountain climbers, cyclists and tennis players, and the revolutionary uniform of the French Resistance. From there it started being worn *à la ville* (in the city) by all genders.

Gabrielle Chanel was one of the first to include berets in her collections during the thirties, praising the simplicity of this small headpiece. Its popularity rose further when French movie star Michèle Morgan wore it in *Le Quai des brumes* in 1938. Gabrielle "Coco" Chanel herself had advised the film-makers, saying: "a movie like this doesn't need any dress: a rain coat, a beret, that's it [voilà tout]". Thirty years

Mythical Staples

Influencer Louise Ebel photographed by Pauline Darley in Paris.

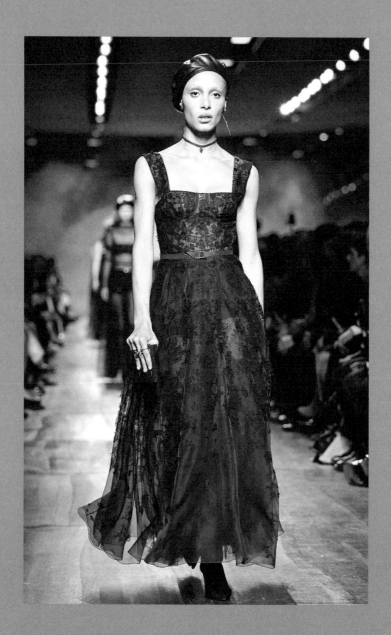

Catherine Deneuve wears a white beret on the set of *Les Demoiselles de Rochefort* by Jacques Demy, 1966.

Adwoa Aboah wears a dark, lacy gown accessorized with a leather beret for the Christian Dior Autumn/ Winter 2017/2018 show during Paris Fashion Week.

later, Brigitte Bardot impersonated a sexy gamine with her brushed bob and black beret in the video for the song 'Bonnie and Clyde'.

A beret is a perfect blank canvas for fashion. It comes in a variety of colours and can be styled any number of ways – straight or sideways, on top of the head or down to the brows – and can be adorned as you please. During the excesses of 1980s fashion, berets were covered in badges and brooches.

In 2017, Maria Grazia Chiuri had the entire Dior cast walk the catwalk wearing black leather berets.

Mythical Staples

LA MARINIÈRE

Whoever has been around Parisiennes for a few days knows that their love for striped tops is no myth.

Horizontal stripes were initially associated with marginalized populations like prisoners or prostitutes . . . and sailors. In 1858, a law made this knit the official base for the sailors' uniform, hence its name *la marinière* (*marin* means "sailor"). Since many French sailors came from Brittany, it became known as the "Breton shirt" in English.

In the twenties, a young Gabrielle Chanel, looking for comfortable and elegant clothes to wear in coastal Normandy, was inspired by the sailor's striped shirts made in comfortable "jersey" (a stretchy knit). She designed her own version and sold it as womenswear in her Deauville boutique.

From the sixties on, designers have played with the French white and navy trademark stripes. Yves Saint Laurent applied them to dresses in his 1966 "Marin" collection. In 1983, the eccentric rising designer Jean Paul Gaultier made marinières the theme of his "Toy boy" collection, starting a trope that would enter his style DNA. He adorns marinières with ruffles, feathers and glitter, and even pairs them with sailor hats. In 2009, at Balmain, Christophe Decarnin created a sequinned, shoulder-padded Breton shirt copied by all of France's top-end high street brands (including Sandro and Maje).

The most timeless marinière is produced by Saint James in Normandy, a company specializing in sailing attire.

Mythical Staples

Coco Chanel and her dog photographed at her home, Villa La Pausa, on the French Riviera, c.1930.

RED LiPS

La Parisienne doesn't wear much makeup except for the occasional bold red lips or black smokey eyes ... says every French makeup artist ever.

The art of colouring lips was familiar in ancient Egypt but disappeared for centuries in Europe because the Catholic church deemed it a sin. Only prostitutes continued to use lip colour.

Lipstick made a comeback in France when Belle Époque celebrities, like actress Sarah Bernhardt, used it to intensify their lips so they could be seen onstage from afar.

In 1870, perfume and cosmetic company Guerlain created the first lipstick – even though wearing any was still considered scandalous. Made with candle wax and pigments, it came in a small case with a slide opening. Over the years, the brand developed increasingly sophisticated methods to apply it, finally creating their iconic "automatic lipstick" in 1936.

In the twenties, avant-garde women like Coco Chanel or dancer Josephine Baker were among the first famous women to make bold lips part of their everyday style. By the end of the thirties, coloured lips had become popular with Parisiennes and several brands had blossomed. Among them, iconic brand Le Rouge Baiser launched a no-transfer formula that was advertised as *"le rouge qui résiste à tout même aux baisers"* ("the red that resists everything, even kisses"). Le Rouge Baiser became a bestseller in France before making its way to Hollywood.

Mythical Staples

Le Rouge Baiser magazine advert from the 1950s.

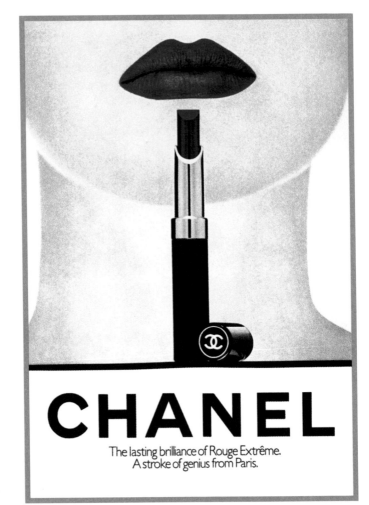

Chanel lipstick magazine advert c.1983.

Juliette Binoche wears a leopard-print
jacket and red lips in Paris, 1991.

In 1940 lipstick consolidated its popularity in France – for the most unexpected reason. After Hitler said he "despised lipstick", Parisiennes coloured their lips as an act of defiance, using beetroot juice when nothing else was available.

"If you feel sad, put on lipstick and attack."
Coco Chanel

After its golden age in the fifties, the lipstick trend had its ups and downs. Less visible during the sixties and seventies – when eyes were the focus – it made a comeback in the last decades of the twentieth century and was most recently popularized by Instagram's "retro French girl" hype of the 2010s.

Search for advice on how to achieve the French beauty look, and you'll find tons of results. According to makeup artist Violette Serrat, French makeup is about enhancing your features rather than reinventing them. And for this, lipstick is the perfect weapon.

As Coco Chanel famously said: "If you feel sad, put on lipstick and attack."

Mythical Staples

THE TRENCH COAT

Androgynous and dramatic, this chic practical raincoat has become a staple of Parisian style, although it was born on the other side of the Channel.

Created in 1820 to withstand the stormy English weather, the water-repellent coat rose to fame when worn by army officers in First World War trenches. Despite being muddied, it was already considered fancy as it was worn only by the upper echelons of the military. Men continued to embrace its panache long after war was over and, noticing this, Hollywood styled it on the most elegant actresses, such as Audrey Hepburn.

The liberated Parisiennes of the sixties, seeking practicality and class, adopted the trench coat. On the set of the 1964 film *Les Parapluies de Cherbourg* (The Umbrellas of Cherbourg), a young Catherine Deneuve defeated rainy Normandy weather while looking adorable wearing a beige trench and a black ribbon in her hair.

The trench coat entered Parisian fashion legend when Yves Saint Laurent designed one for his 1962 collection. With its inherent style and sophistication, the trench has remained in the Parisienne wardrobe ever since. Graphic and knee-length in the sixties, long and thin in the seventies, broad-shouldered and cinched in the eighties ... it adapts to the decade's silhouette. Throw it on and you'll instantly look like a Parisienne.

Mythical Staples

Nino Castelnuovo and Catherine Deneuve walk down a wet
pavement in a scene from *The Umbrellas Of Cherbourg*, 1964.

The white shirt is listed as a wardrobe staple in all "How to dress French" literature, yet this particular look is not easy to master, since the shirt has to be impeccably ironed.

The white shirt's place in the French woman's wardrobe is as the ideal versatile staple. They can be adorned with jewels like the late Coco Chanel, worn open in a sexy manner à la Jane Birkin, or closed neatly in the more restrained style of French-beloved Audrey Hepburn. The collar and sleeves can be used as an embellishment – for example, the iconic black and white contrasting dress designed by Yves Saint Laurent for Catherine Deneuve in *Belle de Jour*.

The diversity of collar styles and shapes is ever-increasing. "Oversized" means cool, "fitted" is more restrained, Peter Pan collars are cute, while the pussy bow look is haughty, ruffles feel glam, etc. This all-purpose basic can be purchased at specialists such as the 1838-founded luxury "*chemiseur*" (shirtmaker) Charvet, located in a mansion in the rue de la Paix, or the 1968-founded Alain Figaret if you have a smaller budget. Many design houses like agnès b. and Yves Saint Laurent always feature a crisp white shirt in their collections. The white shirt is constantly being given a fresh twist: ready-to-wear designer Anne Fontaine has played with its shape and amplified it with multiple embellishments since 1993, while Alexis Mabille has turned it into a couture evening gown.

Parisiennes love a versatile piece and the white shirt is most definitely an excellent base.

A model wears a white shirt accessorized with a tie and bold jewellery for Karl Lagerfeld's Spring/Summer 1987 Chanel show in Paris.

Mythical Staples

SCARVES

The French love their scarves, as indicated in the number of words we have to describe them. For example, there is the "*écharpe*" (thick wool scarf), the "*foulard*" (a lighter scarf, often made of silk or cotton), the "*carré*" (a square silk scarf) and the "*châle*" (shawl).

In the 1800s, aristocrats wore fancy silk scarves neatly tied around their necks. They were mostly manufactured in Lyon, where the silk industry was booming. Meanwhile, working-class men wore similar cotton versions. Originally used to keep warm in winter and soak up sweat in summer, these scarves became emblematic of the working classes.

Scarves became a sophisticated fashion accessory for women in the twenties, worn as a headpiece or around the neck. In 1936, Hermès launched the iconic "*carré de soie*", a square silk printed scarf that became a huge success. The way to wear this symbol of wealth evolved over the years: tied under the chin à la Grace Kelly or wrapped around the hair, turban-style, in the seventies. Since then many types of scarf have been trending: big knits in the eighties, sleek cashmeres in the nineties, thin scarves in Y2K and loose fluid ones in the style of Isabel Marant around 2010.

The art of the French scarf lies in the way you wear it. Seeking answers, *Vogue* published several articles on how to wear a scarf "like a French girl". I would say the answer is not to try too hard, although I do have a few secret tricks of my own.

Stylist Geraldine Saglio's relaxed street style at
Paris Fashion Week, Spring/Summer 2019.

Mythical Staples

SHOULDER AND CROSSBODY BAGS

Parisian cool lies in the ability to move freely without being constrained by clothes, something that shoulder and crossbody bags allow.

Until the 1940s most women's bags were carried in the hand or on the forearm. They were rigid and not very practical. Tired of clutching and losing countless bags, Coco Chanel designed one of the first long strap bags in 1929. Then in February 1955 she created the iconic "2.55" inspired by practical military crossbody bags. Intended to fulfil the modern woman's needs, the straps are long enough to be worn on the shoulders, the fabric is both resistant and soft, while quilting adds volume and comfortable cushioning. It contains seven pockets: the "Mona Lisa smile" curved inner side outer pocket, the centre main folds, a narrow middle fold for lipstick and the zipped inner pocket for more personal items. With such a bag, Chanel could keep her hands in her pockets as she loved to.

Hands-free bag styles are countless, whether luxurious or more affordable. In 1956, Hermès created a daytime "Kelly" bag with a detachable strap, named after Grace Kelly. Since 2013, the "Demi-lune" crossbody bag by Parisian label APC has reached cult status.

The way to carry a strappy bag changes over the years. You can wear it under the arm à la Coco Chanel, low on the hip in a boho manner, tighten the strap for a sporty crossbody look or even wear halfway down the back. It's a quick and easy way to update your style without buying a new bag.

Mythical Staples

A classic but contemporary combination of
beige Chanel 11.12 bag and soft cream knit.

Mireille Darc wears a backless black gown as Christine
in *The Tall Blond Man With One Black Shoe*, 1972.

THE LiTTLE BLACK DRESS

"You are never over- or underdressed with a little black dress," claimed Karl Lagerfeld. Parisiennes love a wardrobe chameleon and the *"petite robe noire"* is the ultimate example.

After the First World War, France was grieving. On the streets, women wore demure black dresses, which would become a symbol of understated elegance. Coco Chanel created her version in 1926: fluid, simple ... the design feels timeless.

Glamorous in the fifties, minimal in the sixties, flowing in the seventies, powerful in the eighties, ultra-light in the nineties, the little black dress follows trends. It can be styled up or down. You may stack layers of necklaces like Coco Chanel, cinch it with a statement belt à la Yves Saint Laurent or keep it clean. Wear it with court shoes in the office, strappy heels at night, and boots or sneakers for a more casual daytime look ... the variations are endless.

Many Parisian icons are famous for their love of black dresses. Chanteuses Edith Piaf, Juliette Gréco and Barbara, "La Dame en Noir" (the lady in black) made it their "forever" attire. Meanwhile, on the sixties big screen, audiences discovered the Saint Laurent demure black dress with white collar worn by Catherine Deneuve in *Belle de Jour* and the fitted dress Jeanne Moreau wore in *Les Liaisons Dangereuses* (1959). Overseas, Audrey Hepburn's Givenchy gown in *Breakfast at Tiffany's* (1961), worn with a rope of pearls slung artfully down her back, became the most famous French LBD in the world.

Mythical Staples

NEUTRAL COLOURS

Parisians sometimes dress as if they are trying to camouflage themselves against the city's beige Haussmannian buildings and grey roofs – hence their reputation for often being stylish yet dull dressers.

But France hasn't always been a land of discreet shades. In Versailles, the royal court of the Sun King Louis XIV was known for its love of vivid colours and shiny fabrics.

However, the tragedy of the First World War brought an end to this colourful era. Grieving women began wearing black dresses, later embellished with sequins as sadness faded to be replaced by a need to party in "*les années folles*" (the Roaring Twenties). Women's fashions had entered the modern age, in all shapes and colours.

With her love of simplicity, Coco Chanel was the emblematic designer of this shift. Fuelled by a distaste for the colours of the Belle Époque, she developed a fashion vocabulary around neutral shades such as beige, black or white. Later, most celebrated French designers would employ a lot of neutrals in their collections: Chloé went for a palette of powdery tones, Céline for beige and soft colours, black was dominant at Yves Saint Laurent and Sonia Rykiel while Isabel Marant opted for more subdued tones.

In a 2015 study, when asked what colour they would be wearing in the coming season, 62 per cent of French women chose neutrals.

Mythical Staples

Caroline de Maigret wearing a tan jacket, nude shirt, beige trousers
and tan bag outside the Haider Ackermann show in Paris, 2018.

THE BLAZER

Since Yves Saint Laurent first inspired them to do so, Parisiennes have been keen to throw a blazer over just about everything for instant chic.

The blazer, as implied by the fact it has the same name in French too, is taken from the English tailoring tradition (as was the trench coat, see page 114). At first the mid-1900s navy uniform, it became the sports jacket of elite university students before shifting to everyday wear. French women were already familiar with jackets after the success of Coco Chanel's tweed versions. When Saint Laurent started twisting traditional menswear into womenswear, Parisiennes were ready to jump on board. From the late sixties onwards, contemporary "effortless" Parisian casual chic was born when stylish young women wore blazers paired with wide-leg pants, jeans and shirts.

And the look hasn't left the Parisian's repertoire. In the seventies it was worn with shirts, ruffles and pussy bows. The eighties marked the time of the "power" blazer: shoulders became wider, colours more diverse. In the nineties, sportswear influences from the US inspired the use of T-shirt layering – a pairing that has become a cult classic – while 2000s blazers grew tighter, influenced by Hedi Slimane's sharp tailored silhouettes. Ten years later, blazers were worn over frilly mini-dresses or with skinny jeans and slouchy T-shirts, as seen in the 2009 Isabel Marant show. For Yves Saint Laurent's "La Parisienne" perfume campaign in 2009, Kate Moss was styled in a black bustier mini-dress with a blazer draped over her shoulders. The blazer still has a key place in our wardrobes today as one of the most versatile jackets you can own.

Mythical Staples

Catherine Deneuve poses with Yves Saint Laurent for the
twentieth anniversary of his fashion house in 1981.

JEANS AND T-SHIRTS

It was about time Parisian fashion was influenced by the US. In the sixties, the globalization of American culture led young Parisians to adopt jeans and T-shirts as staples in their wardrobes.

Created as practical stretchy underwear for the US Navy, T-shirts became popular sporting attire before being associated with rebellious youth in fifties movies. It took actors James Dean and Marlon Brando's undeniable sex appeal in jeans and T-shirts for European hip kids to adopt these trends. Over the years, both pieces lost their rebellious connotations. In the sixties, jeans and T-shirt combos were worn by stylish young women, such as Jane Birkin and Françoise Hardy, yearning for the movie stars' cool. Gradually, the American classics became anchored in the more conservative French women's wardrobes and by the nineties, there was scarcely a Parisian who did not own at least one pair of jeans.

Contrary to many staples that became mainstream after being reinterpreted by a designer (such as the Chanel marinière or the Yves Saint Laurent blazer), jeans and T-shirts have needed no designer interpretation to make it to the high street.

Françoise Hardy wears a relaxed but chic jeans and T-shirt combination in 1966.

Mythical Staples

WALKABLE SHOES

In France, we have a saying, *"être bien dans ses pompes"* (*"pompes"* is slang for shoes), meaning "to be comfortable in your own skin". True to this saying, Parisiennes go for shoes they look and feel good in. French designers André Perugia and Charles Jourdan might have invented stilettos and Christian Louboutin may be the most famous Parisian shoe designer in the world, but Parisiennes, eager not to break an ankle, prefer more comfortable options for everyday life.

For the 1956 movie *Et Dieu... créa la femme* (...And God Created Woman), Brigitte Bardot, who had trained in classical ballet, asked designer Rose Repetto to create a ballet shoe for daywear. Smitten with her *"ballerines"*, the influential actress wore them daily, single-handedly starting a trend. In 1957, Coco Chanel designed her first two-tone slingbacks, the beige body and black tip lengthening the leg while shortening the foot. Then in 1964, Courrèges boots, designed for young fashionable women, with their walkable low block heels and futuristic look, proved a hit. At the same time, more conservative women preferred Céline's classy polo loafers or Roger Vivier's chic low heels.

In the seventies, lengthier pants and dresses called for more height. Yves Saint Laurent had the brilliant idea to add heels to traditional Basque Country espadrilles. The first platform espadrille, developed with specialist manufacturer Castañer, was a huge success. Then in the eighties, sneakers appeared in Parisian outfits. Sometimes imported (Converse or adidas), sometimes local, like the Bensimon canvas tennis shoes – the French counterpart of Converse beloved by off-duty icons Inès de la Fressange and Jane Birkin, who were not afraid to wear them stained. A decade later, students wore chunky Dr. Martens or worn-out sneakers while older fashionistas preferred masculine footwear like loafers or Derby-style open-laced shoes. The beginning of the twenty-first century saw the rise of low-heeled ankle boots such as Isabel Marant's much-copied Dicker boots.

In the 2020s, all these stylish walkable shoes coexist happily on Parisian cobblestones.

Brigitte Bardot on the set of *A Very Private Affair* in 1962.

chapter 4

PARISIENNES

High-fashion star

Cabaret star Josephine Baker had all eyes on her during her shows and beyond. Admired for her outfits, interviewed in countless newspapers, muse of fashion designers, she was one of the first It girls of France's modern era.

Josephine's avant-garde looks were considered shocking by conservatives but met with huge success among hip young women. In 1927 *Vogue Paris* published a picture of a tulle dress "created for mademoiselle Josephine Baker". The following week, many Parisiennes asked their tailors to replicate it. It was the first time a Black woman influenced the French bourgeoisie.

Josephine Baker marketed her image. She founded her own line of cosmetics, whose bestsellers included Bakerfix, designed to master the singer's iconic *accroche-coeurs* (kiss curls).

"J'ai deux amours, mon pays et Paris" ("I have two loves, my country and Paris") sang Josephine Baker in the thirties. Firmly rooted on the banks of the Seine, the Mississippi-born performer was more French than American by the end of the Second World War. When she returned to the United States in the late forties for a series of shows, she stunned Americans in fabulous dresses designed by her friends Pierre Balmain and Christian Dior, thus becoming an ambassador for French couture overseas.

The daring Baker will long be remembered, both as a heroine of the Resistance and as one of the first modern muses.

Josephine Baker photographed in an elegant white
evening gown embellished with crystals, 1951.

The bold elegant

"The most photographed woman in France" was a supermodel before it was a thing. With her cigarettes and red lips, Bettina Graziani was the personification of the sophisticated Parisienne.

Born Simone Bodin in Elbeuf (now Seine-Maritime, Haute-Normandie), the red-headed beauty came to Paris to work as a fashion illustrator in 1943. Instead, she was hired as a fitting model for avant-garde couturier Jacques Fath, who suggested Bettina as a name more suited to a glamorous life. Bettina's beauty, fierce attitude and creativity impressed the most famous photographers. She posed for Irving Penn, Henri Cartier-Bresson, Erwin Blumenfeld and many more.

With her fiery hair, strong red lips and sharp eyeliner, she stood out. For photos, her features were emphasized – for example, her freckles were covered for more contrast on the black-and-white shots. In everyday life, she was more natural, smoked with poise and preferred laid-back garments over the corseted trends of the period. A trendsetter, she dared cut her hair into a garçonne bob.

The French would say Bettina "*avait du chien*", meaning she was bold, irreverent, witty and chic and all of these qualities gave her incredible sex appeal. Almost certainly that mysterious "*je ne sais quoi*".

Parisiennes

Bettina Graziani poses in a dinner dress with a portrait neckline and pleated calf-length skirt for *Vogue* in 1952.

SIMONE DE BEAUVOIR

Eclectic dresser

I'm surprised the famous philosopher hasn't been listed more often in lists of French style icons, as her unique look was the last word in Rive Gauche Parisian style.

"I must tell you that I am not at all interested in clothes," confided the feminist activist Simone de Beauvoir almost at once when interviewed about her wardrobe by Cynthia Judah for the *Observer* in 1960. "I have so many other things to think about, so many other interests that they are not at all on my mind." As Judah commented, "People had laughed at the idea of her talking about clothes, but once de Beauvoir had opened the door of her studio flat in Montparnasse, it was evident that she must have thought about them."

De Beauvoir always wore her hair in a high updo that she would later wrap in a collection of sumptuous scarves. Her outfits were completed by statement costume jewellery – and a lot of it. Also a lover of prints and textures, she would always assemble these in the most tasteful manner. An eclectic buyer, she didn't shy away from incorporating unusual clothes purchased abroad into her outfits. She also wore a hint of blush, lipstick and red nail polish.

In her personal life, her work and her style, Simone de Beauvoir was constantly creating her own path.

Simone de Beauvoir with her signature updo, 1947.

Parisiennes

Fashionable beauty

"Mademoiselle Deneuve", as she likes to be called, is often described as a "cold bourgeoise" since she played such a role as Sèverine in Luis Buñuel's 1967 movie, *Belle de Jour*. The moniker amuses the mischievous actress, but stylewise, this is not far from the truth.

Throughout over half a century of acting, Deneuve's mane of faux blonde hair (yes, she is a natural brunette) has been emblematic of her style. Brushed but never overly coiffed, it represents a more sophisticated take on "French girl hair". Always prepped to perfection, Deneuve embodies refinement.

She is a fashion lover whose style has shifted with trends. Cute and graphic with doe-eyed liner in the sixties, bohemian chic in the seventies, bold and sexy in the eighties, more androgynous sporting shorter cuts in the nineties … no matter what she wears, Deneuve has flair. Friends with many designers, she is often seen in fabulous couture attire. Nothing intimidates the adventurous dresser, who dared to wear her friend Yves Saint Laurent's avant-garde tuxedo in the seventies and doesn't shy away from gold or fuchsia way past her fiftieth birthday.

After four decades of Saint Laurent outfits, Catherine Deneuve sold her couture wardrobe at auction in 2019. The testimony of a fabulously dressed life.

Catherine Deneuve wearing a little black dress, 1965.

Parisiennes

Natural pop star

A truly French talent, the melancholic-looking singer looked natural, even when wearing the most daring couture dresses. At the start of her career, Françoise Hardy was one of the first to rock long, just-got-out-of-bed hair when blow-dried shorter cuts were the dominant sixties trend. She had a discreet attitude, wearing light eye makeup, no visible jewellery and being a bit camera-shy. Indeed, Hardy was the blueprint for the "Parisian cool girl".

When she wasn't on stage, her everyday style consisted of graphic sixties dresses, soon replaced by flared jeans, T-shirts, shirts and and cropped jackets. Françoise always had the cool factor, which made her style look effortless; she also had a love for bright colours that she combined tastefully. Her modern allure inspired a series of young designers, who made her their muse and with her pop-star status, she in turn brought them fame. Françoise was one of the first to wear Paco Rabanne's iconic metallic dress.

As she grew older, she allowed her hair to turn white and had it cut in a short, swooped style, and her style leaned towards a chic androgynous uniform of shirts, jeans and suits.

As a shy 21-year-old, Françoise Hardy confided to *Elle*: "My dream? To look like this image of myself I had a glimpse of as if I was trying my new stage costume. Courrèges. A metamorphosis! Pants and marinière. Blinding white. Daring … like the Françoise Hardy I may one day be."

Françoise Hardy posing elegantly by a window in 1969.

JANE BIRKIN

Nonchalant trendsetter

One óf the most iconic Parisiennes was born in Marylebone, London and still speaks with an adorable English accent despite more than five decades of living in Paris. No matter whether the singer-songwriter and former actress is at a party or strolling through the market, she still looks stunningly *naturelle*. Jane Birkin's effortless style, charming smile and her relationship with singer and provocateur Serge Gainsbourg fascinated photographers, leaving a rich legacy of inspiring photographic images.

Birkin loves natural fabrics and muted colours. She was often seen in wool knits or socks, raw blue jeans, linen blouses, macramé or silk scarves and, of course, carrying that iconic straw basket. Jane's clothes never look "too new". Her daughter Charlotte Gainsbourg (also an actress and singer-songwriter) told *Dazed* in 2017 how she "aged" her clothes: "My mother had a real relationship with clothes which was much more sensual. She used to destroy them – if she had a new T-shirt she would enlarge the collar and make it big." Her long, natural hair, minimal makeup and straw basket made any outfit look natural, even sequins. Always

Jane Birkin with her signature wicker basket while shopping in Paris, 1970.

Parisiennes

"I am English and I come from an environment where I was always comfortable. It matters a lot."

Jane Birkin

nonchalant, she mixed feminine with masculine, fluid with tailored, timeless basics with statements.

As she grew older, Birkin dropped the cute feminine details along with the makeup to focus on bohemian or sporty loose cuts with masculine touches. Forever cool, the British-Parisienne feels like the OG "French influencer" Instagrammers are always eager to emulate.

Looking back on the style of her youth, for which she is still praised today, Jane Birkin has a critical eye, telling *Vogue* in 2019 : "When I see photos of me from 1968, my big doll eyes underlined with eyeliner, exaggerated mouth, bangs, I find it horrible. I found myself the most interesting at forty. I started wearing Scottish cotton marcels, agnès b. men's shirts, oversized pants upgraded with a thin red leather belt and sneakers without laces."

Jane Birkin pictured wearing a statement sheer black minidress alongside then-boyfriend, French singer–songwriter and director Serge Gainsbourg, c.1970.

LOULOU DE LA FALAISE

Influential eccentric

Stylish Loulou de la Falaise found Parisiennes a little dull on arrival in the City of Light. Undeterred, she continued to be her fabulous bohemian self, combining the chic designs of her friend Yves Saint Laurent to create an unforgettably eccentric look that would later influence a host of Parisian women.

On meeting 21-year-old de la Falaise in 1968, Yves Saint Laurent was charmed by her unique bohemian style. Amid still conservative Parisiennes, Loulou, who grew up in London's Swinging Sixties and had just returned from work experience in New York, stood out. Pierre Bergé, Saint Laurent's partner, recalled, "What struck Yves was her extraordinary freedom, she was a bit gypsy and looked like a queen."

Loulou de la Falaise would assemble items she thrifted, choosing shiny fabrics, sultry prints and styling them into magnificent outfits adorned with the most eccentric jewellery. She became Saint Laurent's muse even though she baulked at the label – indeed, she was much, much more! Later hired by her friend, she took charge of the house's jewellery department. In her years there, she made statement jewellery a staple of Parisian style.

Pierre Bergé recalled in a 2012 *Harper's Bazaar* interview: "In many ways, Loulou was the embodiment of the Saint Laurent

Loulou de la Falaise designed jewellery for Yves Saint Laurent, and her own personal style features eclectic accessories and a bright palette.

woman: an impossibly glamorous world traveller, wife and mother who worked full-time at the designer's studio and still somehow found the time to dance on tables at Le Palace."

Loulou de la Falaise brought a hippy glamour vibe from London. In Paris, she made it sophisticated. Hers was a unique style that, through her collaboration with Saint Laurent, would permanently influence les Parisiennes.

FARIDA KHELFA

Alternative muse

If Farida Khelfa's haughty posture remained unchanged since the eighties, her style shifted from punk underground to high-class elegance across the decades.

At 16, Farida ran away from the Lyon suburb where she grew up with her nine siblings to hitch-hike in *direction Paris*. Once there, she hung out at Le Palace, a trendy nightclub where she met up-and-coming designers. The young Jean Paul Gaultier was first to hire her as a catwalk model: "It wasn't only her magnificent features but the way she stood, haughtily, a born aristocrat without an ounce of smugness. I was speechless. Besides, she was super well dressed. The turtleneck, the stirrup trousers, the Creepers, the cinched waist, the pompadour, the hoops ... a true pin-up! [...] I had an instant crush," he recounted in a 2020 interview with *Madame Figaro*. Khelfa then walked for Thierry Mugler, became the muse of photographer Jean-Paul Goude (whom she later had a relationship with) and of couturier Azzedine Alaïa, for whom she modelled before being hired as studio director.

Through the decades Farida, who used to hang out with Paris punks, became "a neo bourgeoise" (as she self-qualifies), who masters the codes of luxurious androgyny. As the first famous model of North African descent, she paved the way for more diversity in fashion, although progress was and is still slow.

Parisiennes

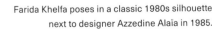

Farida Khelfa poses in a classic 1980s silhouette next to designer Azzedine Alaïa in 1985.

Charlotte Gainsbourg wears a chic white shirt at the premiere for *Les Choses Humaines* in Deauville, 2021.

CHARLOTTE GAINSBOURG

Rock and classic

Charlotte Gainsbourg's minimalist rock twist on timeless classics makes her a contemporary Parisian icon. Style runs through her veins.

Before her thirties, Gainsbourg's look was very simple. In several interviews she confided that she would wear the same jeans, T-shirts, trench and boots day after day for several years. Her encounter with the creative director Nicolas Ghesquière at his Balenciaga show in 2000 marked a turning point in her style. The designer had a crush on her: "I was struck! This girl has unreal grace, elegance and mystery. [...] I felt I met the woman I had been designing clothes [for] forever." The feeling was reciprocal: "I like his modern silhouettes, they look like they have been made for slender girls like me."

Charlotte's friendship with Nicolas contributed to carving out her own sense of style. Now notable for her rock outfits on red carpets – mini-skirts, leather, lamé, tailored shoulders and sexy prints – the once-discreet dresser looks powerful and modern. In daily life she opts for minimal tailored looks, along with cool, timeless classics such as biker jackets, jeans and, still, the trench coat.

Ambassador for many French brands (including Comptoir des Cotonniers and Gerard Darel), Charlotte Gainsbourg has become one of the modern faces of Parisian style.

Parisiennes

LOU DOiLLON

Flamboyant cool

The multitalented singer, illustrator and model is Jane Birkin's youngest daughter with director Jacques Doillon. Lou Doillon's interest in clothes with a patina has been inherited from her mother: "I love clothes that last, that you pass on, that 20 years later you will find in a thrift store," she told *Vogue Paris*. She has an eye for sourcing vintage clothes that fit her folk-rock aesthetic: cowboy boots, biker jackets, flowing dresses and coats. A fan of striking fabrics, even in daytime she sports lamé, velvet, tweed, silk, sheers, lace and embroideries. The eccentric artist also layers delicate jewels like talismans and has a collection of vintage hats and precious scarves.

The stunning brunette, who knows exactly what suits her, opts for dark and rich colours: burgundy, bottle green, night blue, deep purple … lifted with gold and touches of cream. For her silhouette, she mixes tailored masculine lines with flowing bohemian pieces masterfully.

Lou says she is influenced by the zeitgeist, but doesn't follow trends, telling *Vogue*: "French style has got to do with a certain form of arrogance, which I love. French girls have a tremendous respect for themselves in a way, and so they have what they want to wear, and what they won't wear."

Wearing only unique pieces combined in an elaborate manner, Lou Doillon looks so impossibly cool it's hard to copy.

Parisiennes

Lou Doillon wearing a patterned jacket and flared jeans at the 2021 Andam Fashion Awards in Paris.

INÈS DE LA FRESSANGE

Parisian poster child

Chosen by Karl Lagerfeld in the eighties for her resemblance to Coco Chanel, Inès de la Fressange has recently reinvented herself as an international bestselling author with her lifestyle book, *La Parisienne*. Lagerfeld adored Inès's good manners backstage, as well as her wit on the catwalk – the 5'11" brunette would wink at the audience, tell jokes and even smoke.

Like her personality, de la Fressange's look is restrained and witty. When asked to describe her own style, she told *Les Échos* in 2019: "Simple things with sophisticated accessories." An apt description for a woman who pairs high-quality basics with fancy shoes, bags and jewels. She is into androgynous pieces ("I don't look good in frills"), high-quality fabrics, neutral and dark colours, along with the occasional flash of bold colour. To make her simplistic style look high fashion, she relies on layering and accessorizing. True to her own advice, "*Décaler c'est gagné*" ("Clash the styles"), she is not afraid to wear sparkles with a marinière by day and jeans with heels in the evening.

The poster child for timeless Parisian style, Inès's savvy approach means she has turned her flair into a business.

Frivolous, honest and cheerful, Inès de la Fressange doesn't take herself too seriously, which makes her perfect for her self-made Parisian ambassador role.

Inès de la Fressange wearing a tailored navy suit outside the Chanel show during Paris Fashion Week in 2018.

INDEX

CREDITS

The publishers would like to thank the following sources for their kind permission to reproduce the pictures in this book.

Alamy: CBW 15; f8 archive 112; Grzegorz Czapski 28; Ian Dagnall Computing 13; Everett Collection 122, 131; Pictorial Press Ltd 14; Retro AdArchives 22, 111; Reuters 99; Science History Images 21; Zuma Press Inc. 77

Franny Monzemba: 35

Getty Images: AFP 80; /Bruno Bachelet 127; Bentley Archive/ Popperfoto 147; Edward Berthelot 10, 43, 44; Bettmann 66; Edouard Boubat 25; David Cairns 143; Dominique Charriau 88; Christophel Fine Art 39; Robert Doisneau 113; Francois G. Durand 152; Estrop 84; Kurt Hutton 47; Alain Jocard 50; Kammerman 70; Gie Knaeps 87; Patrick Kovarik 83; Reg Lancaster 30; Photo Claudio Lavenia 122, 125; Josse/Leemage 27; Miguel Medina 90; Michael Ochs Archive 115, 135; Mirrorpix 79, 144; Jeremy Moeller 121; Mondadori Portfolio 69; Genevieve

Naylor 54; Irving Penn/Condé Nast 100; Jacopo Raule 157; Suzanne Rault Balet 151; Bertrand Rindoff Petroff 155; Maurice Rougemeont 7; Jean-Claude Sauer 51; Steve Schapiro 128; Pascal Le Segretain 49, 96, 106; Daniel Simon 53, 116; Harrison Smith 149; John Stoddart/ Popperfoto 17; Stringer 60; Philippe Le Tellier 107; Daniele Venturelli 40; Victor Virgile 57, 92, 95

Mary Evans: Glasshouse Images 8-9

Shutterstock: Fredrich Baker/Condé Nast 65; Henry Clarke/Condé Nast 63; Olivier Degoulange 119; Granger 109; Etienne Laurent/EPA 33; Frances McLaughlin-Gill/Condé Nast 136; Deborah Turbeville/Condé Nast 73, 74

Topfoto: /Roger-Viollet 36

Every effort has been made to acknowledge correctly and contact the source and/or copyright holder of each picture and Welbeck Publishing apologises for any unintentional errors or omissions, which will be corrected in future editions of this book.